OLD BLOKE GOES SWIMMING

By

Paul Murdoch

2

Published by NEETAH Books

First printing: November 2021

Copyright (c) 2021 by Neetah Books.

A CIP catalogue for this title is available from the British Library.

ISBN: 978-1-908898-50-0

Dedication

I'd like to dedicate this wee book to my good friend, Sam Kennedy. I'll never forget his wit and wisdom, in and out of the water.

And to my Mum and Dad for all their love in this life.

The Author

Author of '*Old Bloke Goes Running*', Paul Murdoch is a screenwriter, nature lover and musician, with over ten novels published.

www.paulmurdoch.co.uk

1

Old Bloke Takes a Break

In my last book, 'Old Bloke Goes Running', I did exactly that. I explained what inspired me to jog and what gadgets, garb and tricks I used to keep me on the right track. My aim is to do the same here. But first, I should enlighten you a little. Yes, I enjoyed all that running and the shedding of the pounds that went with it. However, after two years of pounding the streets, fields and moors, I began to realise that I might be better diversifying a little. I mean, too much of a good thing can sometimes be a bad thing. Right?

Don't get me wrong, the Grand Master who showed me all the running ropes is still going strong and so was I until… Well… I had a little mishap.

Now sixty, I seem to be prone to more injuries, which is a real pain in the proverbial. Knees going out of kilter, muscles moaning and most recently, an injury that was my own stupid fault.

However, before I go into the gory details of my stumble, I have to say that running was my saviour during the series of lockdowns that befell us in 2020 and beyond. It kept me sane. Even when restrictions were at their tightest, I still donned my togs and did the 'hamster-wheel thing'. You know, fifty-six times round the garden and then back in for my beer and a bath.

When things opened up more, I got out and about as safely as I could. Skirting round other humans while holding my breath, I pounded the empty streets like some post-apocalyptic hero.

Taking to the hills had me in a quandary but, as I wondered about the wisdom of running on some high mountain top, alone and relatively inexperienced, with a myriad of dangers and a very over-stretched ambulance service. I did it once or twice but felt a bit selfish for straying off the straight and narrow.

Up until recently, whenever I overdid it a bit - twisted a knee or pulled a muscle, I'd 'hole up' for a few weeks until my fitness was back and I was ready to overdo it again.

Eventually, during an ill-judged hill run over a mini mountain called Ben Bowie, I pushed myself too far.

I ran across a great stretch of snow and ice, determined to conquer the peak until, right at the top, I took a terrible tumble.

My left foot broke through a thin crust of ice and got trapped in the powdered snow below while the rest of my body continued on.

Poleaxed, and cut by the ice, I crawled to my feet and examined the damage. There was a bit of blood but it was so cold that I didn't feel any pain. So, after rubbing my ankle for a minute, I just got on with it and ran another 8k all the way home.

I was fine for about 48 hours…and then it hit me. My ankle was killing me. I could barely walk and certainly couldn't run. I knew I'd done something, but how could it just suddenly hit me like that?

This was during the UK's second wave of Covid and any thoughts of actually seeing a doctor or going into a hospital seemed like a pipe dream. So, I did my usual...

I hobbled on for a few weeks thinking I would recover again…but I didn't. Another Grand Master, this time of the musical kind, told me I was walking like Quasimodo and that I needed to do something about it. Being a well-read chap, he reckoned it was an instep problem. So, he took me to a chemist and made me buy a pack of rubber insoles. I tried them for a few days but gave up when they seemed to make things worse.

After a month of moaning and a fall from a ladder, caused by my wonky ankle, I took myself to the 'Minor Injuries Department' of my local hospital and got myself x-rayed.

'It looks fine,' said the nurse.

'But I have this feeling of *bone on bone* pain and...'

'It looks fine,' she snapped.

'And my instep is sore which also hurts the tendons behind my knee and...'

'Ok. Here's a number. Maybe you should see a podiatrist.'

I stared at the number wondering why someone couldn't just refer me but, aware that there were *other things going on*, I reluctantly dialled the number. A firm, soulless voice on the other end of the line said, 'Do you have an open wound or a sore oozing puss?'

'Eh, no...' I replied.

'Then I'll put you on the waiting list.'

'Ah... So, how long might that be before I...'

And the line went dead.

After chatting to friends and family, I was informed that 'the waiting list' meant decades rather than days.

So, I thought, what should I do? I'm in pain if I try to run. I'm getting fatter by the day and I'm still on the diet of an 'athlete' - curries, beer and sweets... All things I could get away with when jogging 5-15k every day.

Then I saw an episode of some vet series on the telly where an old stallion, who'd done his knee in, was swimming in this big purpose-built plastic tub. Wait a minute, I thought. That's me!

Right there and then, I hatched a cunning plan...

2

Old Bloke Remembers the Strokes

I first learned to swim when I was five. Hugh Gallagher, a one-time player with the football team, Dumbarton, happened to be a neighbour and I was best pals with his son. Being much sportier than my mum or dad, he took us to the Brock Baths in Dumbarton every week until we could both float without the aid of our rubber rings.

I can still remember clutching my red and white rubber ring in the showers while some older boys laughed behind me. They'd poured carbolic soap over my head which soon found its way into my eyes. It stung so much that I had to run out of the shower and dive back into the pool. I've no idea how I morphed from floater to swimmer. Perhaps it was that painful plunge, but I did and I have to retrospectively thank my childhood pal, Andrew, and his famous dad for that.

Once I could swim, I always found it a bit weird if I met someone who couldn't. It seemed pretty vital for safety reasons and a great shame that anyone would miss out on the fun to be had splashing about in a pool or the sea. As life trundled on, I would discover that loads of people never got around to learning. My mum and the musical Grand Master previously mentioned were amongst their ranks.

My dad was a good swimmer and he used to take my brother and me to the outdoor baths at Helensburgh. That wasn't always such a great experience. It was *Baltic*, as we say here. Absolutely freezin' out of the pool and in the pool. Kids would dive-bomb you from all directions and getting ducked was a common occurrence. No one ever paid much attention to the rules.

Ok, there was usually some stressed-out pool attendant blowing on his little whistle. He might even eject a few ner-do-wells if he could catch them but...it was a bit of a free for all.

There was, of course, the red and black cartoon-like chart on the poolside wall that showed you all the things you weren't supposed to do.

The rule that always caught my attention was the 'no petting' one. This sounded like something you did in a zoo. It should have read – 'no snogging or canoodling'. Anyway, it showed a picture of some dodgy sea-side postcard couple cavorting in the water. I wonder if anyone was actually thrown out for becoming over-excited in the pool?

So, back to the here and now. Luckily, the latest announcement by our First Minister, here in Scotland, meant that swimming pools were back open, albeit in a limited way.

It was time for this 'old stallion' to seek out his swimming togs.

Suddenly, I'm thinking about another Grand Master of the aquatic kind who is, very sadly, no longer with us. Sam knew all the swimming techniques and had the charisma and attitude that totally qualified him to be a guru of the deep.

I must have been in my forties when Sam, an old teacher of mine and eventually a great friend, persuaded me to come along to the baths with him and his 'followers' early one Sunday morning.

Sam would hold court as we swam and chatted our way through sixty-four lengths. The pool was 25 yards long - so that's a mile in *old money*. I called it the 'mile under club'. Forthright and funny, Sam would correct your strokes, no matter if you were seventy or seventeen. He definitely helped me with my crawl and my breaststroke. We'd do three sets of four, an eight and then the same again. After that, we'd do another eight ending with a straight sixteen.

We'd chat between each set of lengths about politics, religion and anything else contentious. Sam was very non-PC, which I loved, and, in the pool with only the bare necessities, there seemed to be a kind of diplomatic immunity that was incredibly refreshing.

Oh, there was one thing that was non-negotiable for any guys in 'the mile under club' - You had to wear trunks!

3

Old Bloke Goes Budgie Smuggling

'Dad!' screamed my oldest daughter. 'Cover yourself up!'

It was Portugal - 2018, and we had a private pool but swimming trunks on a man in his late fifties was apparently a big 'no-no'. Especially as my daughter had her best pal visiting for a few days.

'Wit?' I protest. 'Ye canny get a decent swim in shorts!'

'Well, there's nothin' decent about those!' she blasts, a look of disgust on her gub.

'I think your James Bond days are over, darling,' my better half pipes up.

'I'm not wearing them to impress. I'm wearing them to slip through the water like... like one of them sword fish things.'

'Marlin,' says my younger daughter.

'Monroe?' Now I'm confused.

'Not the actress - the fish!' she explains. 'It's called a Marlin.'

'Oh, aye... one oh them.'

'More like a big eejit,' mutters my better half.

'Budgie smugglers should be banned!' says my oldest. She drags her poor pal away from the poolside, like it's the scene of some heinous crime.

When, I wonder, did a once perfectly normal pair of swimming trunks morph into the pants of Satan? (Okay, so that picture was taken a few years ago… I admit it)

Shamed into donning a pair of shorts, I decide to Google the term 'budgie smugglers'.

'I might have known that the Aussies were to blame for my shame,' I say out loud.

My better half raises her eyebrows.

I read out the explanation that's on the screen. 'Slang for men's tightly-fitting swimwear (trunks), it implies that there is an actual budgie trapped in there instead of…'

'What?' interrupts my better half, already laughing.

'What should be there...' I finish.

My better half is sniggering while sipping a large glass of wine and almost chokes.

'Listen,' I continue, 'if I was going to try and smuggle a budgie, I can think of better places to put it.'

'Why would you want to smuggle a budgie in the first place?' she presses.

'Eww!' Interrupts my youngest girl. 'Will you two stop being sick!'

I raise my hands in surrender before diving headfirst into the pool. Underwater, I realise that I haven't tied my baggy shorts on tight enough. They are now floating somewhere behind me in the gloom and despair.

4

Old Bloke Gets the Gear

Back in the here and now, I think about what I might need to buy. You know, to do the job correctly. I mean, for running, I had to fork out for tons of stuff. Shorts, tops, socks, shoes, headphones, watches…not to mention the various hats, lotions and potions.

Well, I have swimming shorts and swimming trunks. I just have to decide which I'm brave enough to wear. I also have goggles and a towel. Mmmm...? What else? Oh, yes, a swimming watch. Now, a lot has happened since I bought my first running watch. Which, as it happens, could also measure the number of lengths you swam in a pool.

The problem with that watch is that it stopped talking to my phone, which meant I couldn't sync anything, which meant I couldn't chart my 'progress'. It also steamed up. This, I subsequently found out, may have been my own fault. Apparently, you can swim with the watch but not shower with the watch. The steam seems to get into places liquid can't. Who knew? Well, I probably should have, being a science graduate and all that, but Hey-Ho.

'Why would you need a watch to measure how many lengths you swim in the first place?' I hear you say.

Well, it's a bit like spoon-feeding me lyrics via an iPad when I sing live. It's part laziness and part forgetfulness. When I do laps of the pool my mind wanders and I suddenly wonder if I've swum sixteen lengths or twelve. So, I end up doing an extra four lengths just in case. With a swim watch I can relax and just have an occasional glance to see how many I still need to do. Okay. Let's just call it a lazy luxury.

I tried a new watch, but it flickered between the various watch faces with the friction of the water and didn't really suit me. Then I tried another. This one had built-in GPS and was great for running and walking too, giving you maps and loads of data. Ps - I've realised that there's no point in putting pictures of these watches in this book as, five minutes from now, they'll probably be out of date.

This watch had downsides too. It didn't show you the lap numbers, just the distance and it only had one display screen available while you were swimming - and the numbers were tiny. If you could actually see it, it had some useful stuff on there like time taken, calories, heart rate and type of exercise (fat burning, aerobic etc.) However, it was all too small for my old eyes to see clearly, especially underwater through steamed-up goggles.

As with running, someone needs to think of the over fifties and their eyesight. A watch can spout out all the data in China, or even to China, it likes but if you can't see it...

So, give us a bloody big display that counts laps or distance or time (let the user configure what they see) in huge letters!

Then, one night, after a frustrating swim followed by a few wines, I ordered a third watch which seemed to offer some of the things from my wish list. I bid high on eBay and won it.

I forked out £245, and a few days later it arrived.

Once, I'd figured out the various settings and software, it turned out to be 'just the job'. I can configure the display to what I want to see during my swim and, because it is button driven rather than a touch screen, it doesn't flicker off and on in the water.

I settled for distance, time, heart rate and number of lengths - all displayed separately and in big fat letters. Perfect for me. Running-wise, it's also well set up.

Other accoutrements required were goggles and ear plugs. I initially went for a pair of goggles at £9.99. The ear plugs were £4.99 - silicon and for adults.

Both required a good bit of trial and error but the goggles were never perfect, so I upgraded to a pair around the £25 mark and they are much better. They never leak and are clear as a bell.

Details of the swim items I ended up using can be found at www.paulmurdoch.co.uk/old-bloke-goes-swimming

5

Old Bloke Trials the Gear in the Pool

My early experiences with the cheaper goggles weren't good at all. Perhaps it was just the shape of my mush but most of the time, I had one eye filling up with water. This was annoying as it was difficult to judge how far away another swimmer or a wall was. So, you'd end up stopping at every end of the pool in an effort to rearrange the leaking google. Not great when you want to improve your time. I searched for better suction on a different part of my face or pinged the headband higher. Sometimes I tightened them too much and almost popped my eyes out. As I said earlier, spend a bit more on the goggles and get a good fit.

For demisting, I found the best way was to spit on the inner glass then rub it in with your finger.

I did get some looks of disgust as I grogged into my goggles at the side of the pool. Then again, it may have been my budgie smugglers... Note to self - must race into the pool quicker, so other humans don't get an eyeful of my bloaty bod.

Once in the pool, I insert my earplugs, twisting them until they are tight and set my watch to 'pool swim'.

I tried two different plugs for lugs - straight ones and ones with wee flappy bits, a bit like bat wings. The straight ones disappeared after two lengths and the water flooded back into my inner canals. I've no idea where they went to, as every time I did a subsequent length, I scanned the pool bottom and found nothing.

I did hear an elderly lady choking a few lanes away, so it's possible they floated across the surface and down her windpipe. *Oops!*

No... Stick to the plugs that look like bat's wings (depicted). They stay in better and if they do come out, they sink and you can do one of those surface dives and retrieve them.

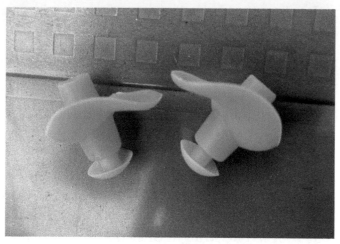

I've covered my watch already. It works well enough. As far as my budgie smugglers go, the swimming Grand Master, Sam, was right. Shorts just flap about like a sack of potatoes and cause massive drag. TRUNKS are best. NO question. They're just, well... A bit embarrassing when you enter the pool and leave for the showers (these days????).

Talking about the showers, I always pop into the loo and pump some soap into my hand from the dispenser thingy. Then, I just slap it on my napper and duck under a nozzle. This saves you from buying expensive shampoo and stuff. We Scots can be a thrifty bunch.

A quick rinse and then a cold stagger into the changing rooms, towel strategically positioned to cover my modesty, i.e. my fat hairy belly and dodgy trunks.

6

Old Bloke Pays for Swimming

The rubbish thing about swimming, compared to running, is that you have to pay money to do it, unless you wild swim, which I'll come onto later. You have to find a pool nearby and acquire a ticket, or a pass etc. You can't just pitch up anywhere and expect to find a decent lap pool. You have to plan ahead, find out opening times and prices. What a pain! All this compared to simply donning some jogging shoes and setting off down any road.

As I was writing this, my better half asked what I was wittering on about this time. In fact, she annoyingly peered over my shoulder and began to read my screen.

'I'm comparing the hassle that comes with swimming to the ease of jogging,' I said.

'Dogging?' she replied, somewhat taken aback.

'Jogging!' I reiterated.

I can tell you here and now, dear reader, that there will never be a sequel to this book titled 'Old Bloke Goes Dogging'. Not unless some huge publisher really 'ups the auntie', so to speak, and offers me a mind-blowing advance.

Even then...

Anyway. Where was I? Oh, yes... Money. But not just money - accessibility.

I'm lucky. We have a 25-yard pool a mere half-mile away. It's a Council pool which means there is a leisure pass that comes in at

£16 a month which, if you do the maths, is pretty good, providing you use it enough.

A one-off swim is roughly £3.50 a go, so if you take a dip five times a week, you've covered the cost with plenty of free swims ahead of you every month.

The trouble with swimming is that there's always something else, some good reason not to bother. It's too busy in the pool. It's my birthday. There's a family 'thing' to do. We're off on holiday. The pool is closed for a water aerobics class... So, hitting my five times a week, never mind a month, is tricky.

There is always the option of joining a private health club. Yes, that's much more expensive but it usually means you have more flexibility because there is greater access. Like, they open at 6.30 am, not 9 am. And they don't close until 10 pm. It all depends on your budget. My local private club is looking for £89 a month.

But does swimming even come close to burning the calories and toning the muscles as much as running? Let's look at that wee conundrum...

7

Old Bloke looks at Swimming vs Running

I've never lost weight by swimming but maybe I wasn't doing it right. Running was fairly easy. Build up slowly and do a bit every day. For me, that meant losing almost three stones. With swimming, the only pounds I lost were the shiny ones, especially from my locker.

Now is as good a time to mention locker thieves. I used to be one myself, so I know what I'm talking about. Let me explain. There are two ways to lose your one pound coin. You know…the one that's needed to operate your changing room locker.

1. You unintentionally leave it in the wee collecting bit and race off outside. After that, it sits for ages until some lucky

person sees it and uses it to lock their own stuff away.

2. You leave it in the wee collecting bit by mistake and go into your cubicle to get changed. This time, there is a whole Bugsy Malone-type kid's operation at play with lookouts and locker collectors harvesting any coins left behind within seconds.

From the coin snatcher's point of view, you're just a kid picking up stuff people have abandoned. The only snag, morally, is that you should have handed that money into reception rather than pocketing it for a sweet shop bonanza.

My sad solution to this these days, as the victim rather than the perpetrator of coin theft, is to have a wee zippy pouch. Inside which I keep my goggles, my bat-wing earplugs, my membership card and my pound coin. I don't leave the building until I check I have all four items safely back in there.

Where was I? Ah, yes…comparing the benefits of running to swimming.

According to the *tinternet* you will lose further weight swimming than running.

What? But I thought…

Well, apparently, you are using more muscles swimming and it takes more physical effort to move the same distance.

And there's the catch... No one is going to swim 5k every day. Right?

Let's compare times then...

Well, according to my watch/workout analyser thing, a twenty-five-minute swim, where I complete 40 lengths (1 km), burns 240 calories. Whereas a 3k run, which usually takes me 26 minutes, burns...wait a minute... The same? So, maybe swimming is better.

On exploring this more, it seems the ratio of running to swimming is more like 4:1, that is, you need to run four times as far to burn the same number of calories. 4 miles running equals 1 mile of swimming.

Swimming is also more of a cardiovascular workout than running and is, quite importantly, less impactful on your old bones.

So how good a swimmer am I compared to other humans?

In 30 minutes...

swimming 20-30 x 25m laps (we say *lengths* in Scotland) is average for a beginner,

40-50 lengths are considered intermediate and

50 or more in 30 minutes, advanced.

At the moment, about ten weeks into my swimming, I do 47 lengths in half an hour. That puts me at the top end of intermediate, which isn't too bad.

To lose my belly fat, however, I need to keep my heart in the fat-burning zone, <112 beats per minute. So far, this is quite difficult as I stray into the aerobic exercise zone, which is more than 112 heartbeats per minute. Perhaps I need to swim more slowly or something.

Comparing running to swimming, however, is still tricky. 'The buoyancy effect' was brought to my attention as some kind of 'put down' on swimming. Personally, I think it's good that you're supported when exercising.

I know most non-swimmers won't believe this, but humans float naturally. You see, the human body has a relative density of 0.98 compared to water. Okay, I guess this does depend on fat, bone density and the salinity of the water, but…

In conclusion, I think I now support 'supported exercise', as picking up injuries while running is the reason I'm writing this book.

So, is swimming better for me now?

Perhaps. But I still miss running.

Calorie loss while swimming also depends on what stroke you do. The butterfly, a stupid stroke in my opinion that must have been invented by a sadist, is best as it crunches the most calories.

Here's a personal summary of the benefits...

Swimming

Can help with joint pain - good, that's what I have.

Can help with mental health – Yes I find it therapeutic.

Can extend life - really? I read that swimming for 30 mins two times a week reduces the risk of strokes and much more. I also read that in a study of over 80,000 people, published in the *British Journal of Sports Medicine* - cycling reduced mortality by 15%, running by 'not a lot' and swimming by 28%!

Can strengthen your lungs - Good. I have asthma. However, I have to say that running also really helped my asthma. After about a year my flow meter reading was almost normal.

Can make you younger - where do I sign?

Can be fun - can be... but not always. See the next chapter...

Can make you a better runner - who knew? However, this may be my final cunning plan. To combine both…

Can be done indoors, no matter what the weather outside - I have to admit that I loved running in the rain.

Running

Kick-starts your metabolism and burns fat - I do think this is still true. When I was running regularly, I could pretty much eat what I wanted.

You get 'runners high' - Yep. Had this. Running is very addictive. Whenever I picked up some injury and had to pause my running, I'd look at other runners with complete and utter envy.

Helps build bone density as it's weight bearing - probably a good thing unless too much weight is bearing down on them bones and you do yourself an injury.

Good cardiovascular exercise - so is swimming, and probably more so.

Easy to do anywhere - hats off. True.

Helps you sleep better - I'm guessing most exercise does this.

Improves immunity - regular moderate exercise is apparently better than occasional extreme exercise, which can lower immunity.

I guess, if you can do running in moderation and swimming, then - you may get the best of both worlds. Don't even get me started on cycling. That's a whole other book.

8

Old Bloke Heads for the Pool in Earnest

I'm sure there was a bit in the last swimming list that said 'swimming was good for your mental health'. Yes, but I can also get annoyed or even ragin' while swimming, which I'm guessing, *isn't* good for your mental health.

But how could sailing up and down the pool, gracefully cutting through the water like *Flipper* possibly get you annoyed? I hear you say.

Because, unless you are 'minted' and have your own 25-meter lap pool, swimming involves sharing a reasonably confined space with other humans. And it's not just in the water that you might want to *blooter* someone - the aggravation can start way before that.

Outside the pool building...

Let's start with the 'early bird'. You know, the guy or gal that always gets the nearest parking space to the pool reception and is already loitering at the doors before they even open. It's kind of okay if there is just one of them but when you see a big queue outside the pool, you can do one of three things:

Say, sod it, turn the car around, and race back home in a huff for a fry up.

Analyse the competition. How old are they? How big are they? What size of bag do they have? - What you're doing here is deciding who you can beat into the pool. Because, first in gets the best spot, like a lane beside one of the sides. This means fewer people to navigate around when you do those lengths. You count the number of people in the queue and deduct 'the weak' and 'slow changers' from the competition. If there are too many fit people ahead of you, you'll probably want to resort to option 1.

Accept your fate and realise that you're going to have to zig-zag through a melee of splashers, chatters and thrashers for however long it takes you to complete your swim regime.

Let's move inside the building.

The reception area...

So, you're through the door but there's still a queue at the till. People can't find their one pound coins. Someone's forgotten their towel. Someone's membership card isn't working. Meanwhile, valuable swim time is ebbing away. You spy the automatic membership card reader and duck sideways towards it but some other 'Old Bloke' gets there first.

It typically takes seconds to flick your card under the infrared reader and select the 'collect ticket' button but no... the guy in front is an *automatic card reader virgin*. He presses all the buttons and steps back to see if it works. He inserts his card in the ticket slot. He bangs the machine twice and curses.

Usually, I would dive in and help him but he's boiling with rage, and it's still 'Covid central' in our area. We're still all wearing masks and supposed to be socially distancing. So, I make an executive decision and walk straight into the changing rooms. I'll use my card on the way out, I decide.

Speaking about my card...

Let me quickly rewind to obtaining my membership card. I tried to do it online but after entering my email forty times and re-entering all sorts of details to no avail, I threw my phone across the room and gave up.

I eventually bought my membership the old-fashioned way. I spoke to the receptionist. *(Ps-I must say that all the receptionists at my pool are top-notch. Nice people).* It was easy to join this way.

"Fill this form in and I'll have your card ready when you come out," she said.

And so, the pass came to pass...as it were.

The changing rooms... part 1 (going in)

Once I'm opposite a locker, standing in a heat haze of disinfectant, I whip off my mask and feel so relieved that I have my wee pouch. You know, the one that contains my pound coin, goggles, card and earplugs.

In days gone by... If I ever did forget my pound coin, I'd simply trust my smelly pants and socks to fate and take my towel to the poolside, my keys and dosh rolled up inside.

9

Old Bloke Gets Wet

In the pool...

Where do I begin?

The biggest problem, and I know I'm being mildly selfish, is getting enough space to swim in a straight line from one end to the other without having to stop, deviate or give up altogether.

Look, I know there are more important things than me getting my lengths in. Children playing and getting to love the water, nanas nattering, papas plunging and mums meandering but...

In 'the old days', there used to be certain times you could do laps and with specific lanes sectioned off. I'm sure that will all come back one day but in the meantime, here's a wee list of typical pool-goers:

<u>The Lapper</u> - just wants to clock up the lengths in a boring methodical way. Often seen checking their watch and the pool clock. (Me)

<u>The Natterer</u> - they usually come in pairs; often but not always, two ladies doing a languid breaststroke, much more interested in chatting than lapping.

<u>The Stormtrooper</u> - usually male and middle-aged, they plough a mean furrow through the water at ramming speed and give no quarter to man, woman or child. (Not me)

<u>The Dabbler</u> - a man, a woman but, more often than not, a child in a little world of their own. Holding onto the edge then swimming in circles with the odd surface dive thrown in. They are blissfully unaware of other humans in the pool.

<u>The Zig-Zagger</u> - they look as if they are doing laps but have no sense of direction. Their

inner gyroscope is defunct and they have no idea that they have crossed four lanes in their effort to complete a single length.

The Competitor - usually another, much quicker, lapper who wears a swim hat and moves like an Olympian. They are usually tucked into the side of the pool, resolute and inwardly smug that they are kicking your ass each time they wiz past you. Often performs an underwater turn at each end.

The Lane Switcher - usually a restless soul who can never get a straight run and continually changes their position in the pool to try and find the best route.

The Usurper - someone who gets into the pool and starts swimming at any point they choose regardless of who is already doing stuff in that space. All of the above have to scatter to make way for this person and who is secretly hated. A kind of 'group resentment' begins to diffuse through the water like poison.

The Challenger - someone who calls anyone to account for disturbing their swim. This may be of their own volition, but more-often-than-not it's at the behest of their better half. 'That's the third time that old git has bumped into me. Are you going to say something or what?' ...kind of thing.

The Tell-Tale – a nosey person who sees someone misbehaving and tells the lifeguard.

The Splashy Kid - there are two types: a) the unaware - they dive in anywhere regardless of who is swimming where and throw heavy rubber sticks anywhere they like with the notion that they may dive down for them at some point. This means they can hit you from above or below. b) The partially aware - they are playful but respectful of other people's space. They may still cut across your path but are more likely to use the word 'sorry' as a kind of 'trump card' that cancels out any misdemeanour.

There is a big, big proviso here - everybody has a right to use and enjoy a public pool. Especially children who, through play, become better swimmers and more confident in the water. They deserve a good bit of leeway in my book, but swim attendants should be observing them carefully.

My tip for swimming a little more peacefully, when children are about, is to switch from wall hugging to lapping in the middle of the pool. Children inevitably dive in a lot and therefore continually use the stairs and race back to the sides.

Before I climb out of the pool of my own volition, there is one specific situation where you may need to make a sharp exit. *The floater* is, thankfully, an infrequent visitor to the municipal waterways. However, I do remember an incident in a lazy river when our whole family, gently bobbing along on various inflatables, were overtaken by a little foreign body. The panic that ensued was frightening. There is only one thing that will vacate a swimming pool quicker than a wee jobby, and that's a Great White Shark. Both will strike an equal amount of fear in the chest of any swimmer.

Never use the pool as a toilet, even for a harmless tinkle, and if you have very young kids, make sure they're wearing the best waterproof nappies money can buy.

In the showers...

There is actually some confusion just now as to whether people are even allowed to shower in these COVID days but, in normal times, showering can be the main event for some people.

They have two towels and a concoction of shampoos, conditioners, lotions and potions piled at their feet as they lather up. They often spend more time under the showerhead than in the pool.

I always seem to get the schizophrenic shower that can't make up its mind whether it's ice cold or scalding hot, so I spend my time, and probably some extra calories, jumping in and out of the unpredictable jet stream. I have, of course, forgotten to take my shampoo or soap, so look on with some jealousy at everyone else.

As I said previously, there is usually some kind of free soap in the poolside toilets, which is fair game - but have you ever been tempted in the showers..?

Some ultra-organised swimmer has left their posh dandruff shampoo at the edge of the shower room. It's just sitting there and you're all alone. What do you do?

It was just a wee squeeze, your honour. No harm done. Unless they come back and catch you 'in flagrante delicto'.

Here's how to get out of that one:

'Eh... is that my shampoo you've got?' says stranger.

'What this?' you enquire, squinting down through soap-filled eyes.

'Aye. That!' they say.

'Oh, I thought someone had left it behind...' you say, innocently.

'But- '

'There you go. Ta.' you interrupt, politely.

And then grab your towel and walk briskly into the changing rooms.

The Changing Rooms, part 2… (coming out)

There's a row of a hundred empty lockers in the way in for your swim so, you pick one and that's that. On the way out, there are now ninety-eight free lockers. Only, the other occupied one is right next to yours…

You're shivering and dripping - and now someone is loitering, half-naked, right in front of your stuff!

Then, as most of the changing booths are taped over for social distancing, the nearest one is almost a block away. This means you have to make multiple return trips, cold and wet, only to discover you've left a soaking wet sock somewhere in no man's land.

Things I realise I've forgotten or lost after a swim - when safely inside my cubicle:

Underpants - solution - *go commando*.

Socks - solution - *go sockless*.

Towel - solution - *dry yourself with your shirt or jumper*.

Shoes - solution - *pretend you're a hippy and walk out barefoot*.

The Car Park...

Ideally, a place you walk through after your swim, as you've left the car at the house and jogged there.

I try to do this as much as possible, but sometimes other things need done before and after and... I know, more pathetic excuses... So, I take the car.

Anyway, you wave bye-bye to the attractive receptionist, all cool and clean, before smacking your face off the automatic door that doesn't quite open the way it should. You regain your composure and then step outside into God's own air. There's a spring in your step and a glow about you as you wander over to the car. I always chuck my wet togs (towel and trunks) onto the front window sill, especially if it's sunny. Open everything up and let it dry in the baking heat beneath the glass. Why pay for radiators and spin driers? I reckon a pair of trunks can be recycled this way about seventy-three times before you need to throw them in the washing machine.

Then it's off to the shop for some square sausage, croissants and black pudding... Or is it? You'll have to wait and see when I go through my swimming regime a few chapters on.

10

Old Bloke Goes by the Book

I bet you're wondering what I mean by the chapter heading above. Let me tell you a story...

About five years ago, I had a chat with an older lady, probably in her seventies, about her swimming. She'd spoken to me at the reception desk a few times and I'd noticed that she was a really good swimmer.

'So, when did you learn to swim,' I asked, as we waited to get into the pool building.

She smiled and said, 'Not as long ago as you might think.'

Deciding that she took my question to be more about her age than her swimming ability, I backtracked. 'No, I didn't mean...'

'Only about ten years ago,' she interrupted. She was as sharp as a tack and seemed to be enjoying my awkwardness.

'Ten years ago?' I pressed.

'From a book,' she continued. 'I was sixty-two at the time, in case you were wondering.'

'No, I wasn't wondering.'

'Yes, you were.' She smiled mischievously. The main doors had opened, and we moved a little closer to the reception.

'So, how could you possibly learn to swim from a book?' I enquired.

'No one ever taught me to swim when I was young. It wasn't that popular where I came from. However, I moved to Majorca to retire when I was sixty and wanted to make the best of it.'

'So, were there diagrams and stuff or…'

'Yes. And a few instructions,' she added. 'I placed it beside the edge of the shallow end of the municipal pool and splashed around, referring to my slightly damp book as and when required.'

I suddenly thought back to the first time our flat coat retriever, Sophie, had taken to the water. She'd followed her mum into a deep river and went straight under, like a hippopotamus, her feet treading the river bed.

Totally taken by surprise, I jumped in after her and managed to catch her collar.

Sophie had no reason to believe that she couldn't simply carry on breathing and running under water. I yanked her to the surface and, bit by bit, she copied her mum and got the hang of the doggy paddle.

'So, was it the doggy paddle?' I asked.

'It was supposed to be the breaststroke, but I found it hard to keep my head above the water and do all the movements at the same time,' she said. 'So, I realised that it might be easier if I put my head under and tried.'

I was beginning to think she was 'taking the mince', but then she got all serious and said, 'It wasn't about learning to do a stroke as such, at least in my experience. It was about overcoming the fear of drowning. Once I'd worked out that, in the shallow end, I was simply swimming in waist-high water. I wasn't going to be out my depth as long as I did breadths not lengths. I practised putting my face under. I got goggles and just submerged myself and allowed myself to float back up to the surface. Then I added a few doggy paddle-type strokes.'

'So, the book became redundant,' I pressed.

'No. After I had some confidence, I reread the book's instructions and applied them.'

'But you swim great. I've seen you.'

She laughed and pointed at a sallow-skinned man in the car park. 'I met my husband, Miguel, at the municipal pool. He used to tease me about my book, and eventually he taught me the techniques I use now. The book brought us together.' She eyed me and nodded. 'You need to lift your elbows out of the water more during the crawl and roll equally.'

'Equally?'

'You roll to your right as you straighten your right arm, but you only half commit to your left arm stroke. Roll equally!'

And she was right. When I did as I was told, my pace improved and I felt more balanced in the water.

It was nice, I thought, that the book did two things for her. It taught her to swim, and it got her a husband.

The strange thing is, after our one-off chat outside the pool, I never saw her again. Which was sad. No one seemed to know who she was and, maddeningly, I'd never asked her what that book was called.

11

Old Bloke Swims Outside

Freezing is the word that comes to mind when thinking about swimming outside. The concept was first introduced to me by my dad, who took me to an open-air pool in the sixties. The sky was overcast and the water looked cold.

'It's fine,' he said. 'The pool's heated.'

He lied! The water was absolutely 'Baltic' as we say here. My whole body went numb.

'You'll get used to it,' he said.

He lied again! I didn't get used to it at all.

Of course, as I grew up, I went with my pals to the various local swimming haunts. The local rivers and lochs were 'Baltic' too but you had to pretend they weren't, just to look cool... Whether it was diving off the pier next to the

Maid of the Loch Steamer in Loch Lomond or braving Craig's Pool in Glen Fruin, you had to smile and say, 'it was great'.

All dangerous stuff when you look back on it now. My mum used to say the 'Loch' takes seven lives every year' ...and she wasn't wrong. The thing about random outdoor swimming is that you can't account for underwater currents, underwater objects or the sheer stupidity and bravado of young kids. Hands up. I did it. I got lucky. Many didn't.

Learning to swim is a given these days but teaching kids how to keep safe is still a challenge.

My kids were taught in our Council pool by some magnificent teachers there. They all had the perfect mix of patience and assertiveness.

As a youngster, my first 'near-death' experience was in my own backyard. There was a big old sink outside that filled up with rainwater. I'm guessing it was used for the plants in the garden. Well, I was only one and barely walking when I toppled in. I think I have a vague recollection of bubbles in the darkness.

My panic-stricken dad hauled me out, but others haven't always been as fortunate. Keeping places safe for kids is so important.

Nowadays, some of the best times in my life are when I'm swimming outdoors. Okay, probably in the Mediterranean Sea rather than in a cold Scottish loch but it still counts. It can be bracing when you first edge yourself in, but soon you acclimatise and it becomes *so* refreshing.

Unless you are on a Greek island near a turtle's nest. Let me explain...

About a year into my running fad, we went on holiday to Kefalonia. Heaven on Earth, as far as I'm concerned. Clear water and hot weather. Even more fabulous was the way I'd planned my morning run. I always ended up in this idyllic little cove at about eight in the morning.

We'd stumbled upon a naturist beach by mistake early in the holiday and, after racing past as quickly as we could, averting our eyes, we found an idyllic cove right at the end of the nudie section. So, we went in – albeit wearing our swim costumes. It was great until my better half began to make some funny wee noises.

'What's wrong, dear?' I enquired.

'It's...' She looked down and yelped. 'It's the wee fish. They're nibbling my legs and feet.'

'Ah!' I gasped. One of the tiny terrors had just bitten me too.

It was fine if you were moving, but if you stopped for any length of time, they'd gang up on you, like a pack of piranhas and attack.

We dashed back to the shore in seconds and wondered what kind of fish would do such a thing.

Anyway... my run ended up at the same cove every day and, as no one was ever about, I'd whip off my running stuff and dive in for a refreshing skinny dip. As long as I kept moving, I had no piranha problems.

However, one morning, I stripped off and dived in as usual, only to find myself trapped.

Some older, clothed people had appeared in *my* cove. They were only feet from my abandoned clothes. I couldn't get out of the water. The longer I loitered, of course, the more I felt the odd random nibble. What was I to do? Wait in the water until the people left the beach and risk a full-on nether region attack or walk out as if I wasn't in the least bothered about being naked?

Two more minutes of providing breakfast for the hell fish and I was out of there.

The people on the beach made way as I politely nodded at my clothes and said 'excuse me.'

Fumbling to get dressed with my wee audience, I jogged off with as much pride and dignity as I could muster. Which wasn't much.

Damn those turtle nest scientists!

Other incidents while open water swimming have been - almost getting attacked by sharks...almost getting attacked by sharks and almost getting attacked by sharks.

Like everyone else in the 70's watching the film 'Jaws' really put a damper on swimming in the sea. But my first dalliance with a demon from the deep was actually Pre-Spielberg.

On a paddle boat with my dad and best friend in Majorca, we had almost lost sight of land when I decided to begin diving off the boat and then climbing back in again. My dad seemed relaxed as the water was calm and we had fun until, all of a sudden, I caught sight of a big shadow going under the boat.

Perhaps nine or so feet long with a funny hammer-shaped head, it was pretty distinctive.

A big fan of the Jacques Cousteau TV series, my mate shouted, 'Hammerhead shark!'

Almost instantly, dad's look of 'stop winding me up' changed to one of 'let's get the feck out of here!'

I've never travelled on a faster pedalo since. We made that beach in about a minute and a half, ploughing up the sand like a Viking long ship - scattering sunbathers and pedalo attendants as we shuddered to a stop.

My second shark encounter was off the coast of Santorini. I know. I'm a name dropping, spoilt git, but I'd worked like a Trojan all summer for that holiday. One day, snorkelling quite far out from the beach my sunburnt mate and myself spotted a reef. We hovered over it in wonder, dazzled by the hive of activity in front of us. The crystal-clear sea was filled with a myriad of tiny fish, a living montage of colour, while behind us the waters faded into a deep inky black.

One second, my splashing companion was right beside me, the next, he was gone. I spun round, treading water as I scanned the horizon. 'Derek!' I shouted. Then I saw him, about a hundred yards away - making for the shore in a frenzy of foam.

Paranoia kicked in and I peered back into the inky depths. In an instant, a wave of fear engulfed me and I pounded through the waves like a Mississippi steamer.

Panting and spluttering I soon stood over my 'life-long pal'. 'What happened to you?' I wheezed.

He looked a bit crestfallen. 'I thought I saw...'

'What?' I pressed.

'A shark,' he muttered.

'And it never occurred to you, not even for a nano second, to warn me? Tap me on the shoulder and say, we better swim for our lives?'

'I... it all... it might not have been...'

'Thanks, mate!' I blasted.

The third and last time I almost encountered a 'Nobby Clark' was in Bali. I know, I know... I can't help it. I was working. Still. It was a roasting hot day and after a four-hour drive through a jungle in the middle of nowhere, I wandered off and jumped into the sea. There was no one around. Just some fishing boats and me on this black volcanic beach. It was wonderful... I floated in the choppy little waves and cooled down beautifully. Bliss.

That night, the humidity was through the roof and I was sweating like a fat lad in a spin class. So, I excused myself from our card game and wandered back towards the sea. It was then that our local guide said, 'Where are you going, Paul?'

'For a dip,' I replied.

He stood up, all agitated.

'Not in there my friend. The sharks come in shore at night.'

I dropped my bathing towel. 'Did you say sharks?'

'Yes, my friend,' he confirmed.

'But I was in there today,' I added.

He smiled. 'You got lucky.'

Anyway, enough of my foreign open water tales. I know lots of people don a wet suit and 'Wild Swim' in Loch Lomond or in the Firth of Clyde. So, I thought it only fair that I give that particular form of self-torture a go…for the sake perspective.

12

Old Bloke Goes Wild

This chapter would never have been written if it wasn't for my better half's eternal quest for a bargain. She had the chance to buy a wet suit for £40 and went for it.

"So," she said. "How does it look?"

I had to admit that the words 'Bond' and 'Girl' did flutter into my head for a bit. So, I began whistling that famous theme tune, only to receive a swift kick to the shin.

"So, when are you getting yours she added?"

Browbeaten, I looked online and found a similar suit for a similar price. And that was brand new. So…when we next went south, to Newton Stewart not Nice, we jammed ourselves into the black rubber gear and drove to a nearby beach. We'd seen some other old bloke wade into the sea at the same spot a few days before so, we reckoned it might be safe.

The only thing was, we stupidly picked a day that was much, much colder. There were hailstones ricocheting off my skull and the

wind was up. Ginormous waves were crashing over us as we chittered our way in.

Being my first ever time in a wet suit, I soon found out that the wet bit means that you still get wet...and hence ice cold. I literally screamed when the Irish Sea reached my nether regions.

This, of course, made my better half yelp with glee. She does that, you know. Whenever I hurt myself – bang my head, jam my finger or trip, she erupts into uncontrollable laughter.

If I could just find a way to perpetually maim myself, I would have a very happy marriage indeed…

Anyway, things weren't getting any better. Now my naked hands were painfully cold and water was rushing down my neck.

"You'll get used to it," she giggled.

"No, I bloody won't," I moaned. But I did. And before long the layer of water next to my skin actually became warm and I was fairly comfortable. My naked hands, however, felt as though they were being frozen off.

Because I had my rubber shoes on, my feet were warm but they kept floating up, tipping my head down. Eventually, I found a way to swim, or at least move forward through the waves. Before long, I was actually enjoying it.

Down at sea level, birds seemed to ignore me and I saw skeins of geese gliding over the ocean...oystercatchers skimming past me through a hoary haze of spray... A crack in the clouds appeared and the sun's winter rays shone down like celestial spotlights on us and... Well... It was lovely. We laughed. We splashed about. And all was good...

We'd waited until the beach was clear before venturing in but now, a sizeable cluster of dog walkers had gathered to watch us.

"You go in first," my better half panted. "Distract them with your big belly while I sneak up the other side of the beach."

"Charming!" I chittered.

But I did, and it worked. Before long, we were both back at the car trying to peel off our fake blubber without revealing too much of the real stuff to the elements or the onlookers.

I got into a right fankle and almost toppled over before giving up and placing a poly bag on the driver's seat.

"Right," I said. "Time to make a quick exit."

And we did. With the blower on warp factor 9 and the heated seats on high. It felt great. Like we'd pulled of a heist... Driving off, still dripping…still full of exhilaration.

After that, we made a pact to do more wild swimming. We'd buy a day-glow bag/float thing and a pair of neoprene diving gloves…

We'd even check the tides and the water temperature. All available online.

This is the sea temperature chart for our little bay.

Summer – 14 -16 degrees

Autumn – 10 -14 degrees

Winter – 8 -10 degrees

Spring – 6 - 14 degrees

Actually, March seemed to be the coldest month, so I might give it a miss then.

Without a wet suit, you might be unconscious in a few hours or even a few minutes so, best check those temperatures first.

Note – freshwater lochs are consistently colder than the sea, I'm told.

How cold can you handle it in a wet suit?

It all depends on the thickness - 7mm, you can probably go down as far as 0 degrees Celsius. 2mm, and you might start shivering at 19 degrees Celsius.

Without a wet suit they say 20-15C is dangerous and 15-10 is very dangerous.

Always factor in currents and tides and probably join a local wild swimming club or at least go with someone who's done it before.

Oh… there are pics of all my rubber gear at

https://www.paulmurdoch.co.uk/old-bloke-goes-swimming

13

Old Bloke's New Swimming Regime

Back in the land of the indoor public swimming pool... Here's what I do.

I know it's not everyone's cup of tea but dawn is my favourite time of day. And just as well, because a swim before breakfast helps keep the calories off.

So, you made it to the start of another day and it's time to slip out of bed and grab your pool bag. I always keep mine packed and at the ready. I have my zip pouch with my goggles, ear buds and pound coin; my towel (sometimes still damp from the day before but I'm working on that) and my trunks. I've talked about my trunks already but my towel is also worth a mention.

Have you ever seen the bit in 'Planes, Trains and Automobiles' where Steve Martin tries to have a shower and is only left with something the size of a face cloth to dry himself after John Candy has used everything else? Well, I don't actually believe you need much more than that to dry yourself.

My better half will, of course, lug around at least two towels - one for her hair and one for her bod. But me... I'd rather travel light. A hand towel does me fine. Less to carry, easier to wash and dry, less hassle prising it in and out of your swim bag. And if you use it properly, you can get dry enough to wrench on your socks, haul up your pants and struggle into your t-shirt, no bother...

So, back to the regime... I used to jump into the car but, the more I hear about climate change, the more I'm inclined to walk or jog to the pool instead. It's only 1km from my house so, 'I'm just being lazy and killing the planet' if I don't.

I'm quoting my 'better half' there. However, I have a wee inkling that she just wants the car for herself.

Anyway, I guess those two extra kilometres walking will actually burn off more calories and let me eat an extra slice of toast on my return.

Once at the pool, I slip into my usual routine.

Which is? I hear you say.

Which is - to put on my gear and plank my locker key in my tiny towel before wedging it above a heater beside the water, where I can see it.

I quickly turn on the shower and shimmy through the cold spray before getting poolside. Then, I cross no man's land before doing a kind of feet-first flop into the pool. I don't want to startle too many people. (Fat old bloke in budgie smugglers warning!)

I pick my spot as I check my watch and set it to 'pool swim'. Then I hit 'Go' and kick off.

I've played around with different screen settings and lap measurements and settled on three screens… Number of lengths, number of metres and heart rate. Why heart rate? Well, I like to check that I'm not going over my max heart rate for my age.

Your watch will calculate it for you if you put your age in there but if you want to work it out yourself, you just subtract your age from 220. In my case, 220-60 = 160 beats per minute. Anything over that, for too long, and I might be overdoing it.

I occasionally stray into the danger zone. If so, I slow down a bit or float face down for a few seconds to see if the lifeguard is paying attention.

Only kidding!

Everyone needs to find their own pace and the number of lengths that suits them. Do an amount that feels comfortable at first and then try to add a few extra on every week. I started off at 30 lengths, which took me about 20 mins and then I was out. Now, a good few months in, I'm doing 50 lengths in about 30 minutes. I've increased my time and my lengths. I sometimes do a mile, which is 64 x 25 metres, but only if the pool is quiet.

I've set my lap time to 30 mins. So, my watch vibrates and I can see if I've hit my 50 length target or not. Sometimes it's 47, sometimes it's 51…

Remember to save your swim on your watch before you come out of the pool. There's nothing worse than driving or walking home while your poor wee watch is having a mental breakdown trying to work out which stroke you're doing and how fast… you're suddenly at 112 lengths and you have to delete the whole dang workout.

To any passers-by who have seen me ranting at my right wrist, calling my watch everything…this is exactly what has happened.

Ideally, I save both 1km walks and my 1.25 km swim. Total calories burned are around 500 and I may still go for other walks or even a run later.

You see, by the time I'm writing this particular paragraph, I'm gently breaking myself into running again. Only 2 or 3 km at a time and only some days…

Apart from my exercise regime, I have also looked at my eating habits and yes...my average number of beers in the bath...

14

Old Bloke Eats, Drinks and Swims

Chilling at a family barbecue, I decided to do a wee survey. The better halves had split off into their wee coven and it was just us old blokes left at the table.

'So, how's the swimming going?' asked one old Bloke.

'Well, it's going just fine,' I replied, sounding a bit like Stan Laurel.

'But you still seem…' the second old Bloke hesitated as he surveyed my belly, '…to still be a bit on the-'

'Chubby side?' I interjected.

Both old blokes took a sip of their beers and looked at each other.

'So, tell me,' I prompted, 'how much do you each drink in a week?' I knew both had medical conditions. I have a few myself - high cholesterol and a few other bits and bobs in need of attention.

We were all very truthful with each other and the weekly units for all three of us averaged out at 50! And that was each, not between us. It was time to reel it all back.

Food-wise, various Covid lockdowns have taken their toll on my willpower, boredom thresholds and waistline. I was comfort eating without exercising (due to my ankle injury). Chocolates, nuts, and pastry had all found their way back into my cupboard via that, all-too-easy, online shopping basket.

I hate to say this, but I'm betting the knock-on death toll from Covid could be much more far-reaching than anybody thinks just now.

I hadn't quite regained my pre- 'Old Bloke Goes Running' weight of 15 stone 6 but I wasn't far off it, at a whopping 14 stone 7. As soon as I began running a little, I dropped to 14 stone. And that was within two weeks.

So, what to do?

I began weighing myself every day and, of course, my daily exercises were building again, but the booze and the junk would have to be reined back.

Two days a week, I would stick to 700 calories, avoid carbs and chuck the chocolate muffins, so to speak. I also upped my fruit and veg intake.

I'd knock the wine intake back by three bottles a week. That's half of what I used to drink and I'd have four drink-free days. I know… not perfect, but realistic. I like wine with fantastic food - and fun still has to be a part of my life. I was also experimenting with a few home-grown recipes that I really enjoyed. (Three examples coming up soon)

Here are a few of the changes I made...

Replacement therapy...

Potatoes out... Sweet potatoes and aubergine in.

Fried rice and Nan bread out... Grated cauliflower and bean sprouts in.

Chocolate and biscuits out... Fruit and Greek yogurt in.

Ribeye steak out... Fillet steak in.

Sugary breakfast cereals out... Mushroom and chilli omelettes in.

Dry roasted nuts and crisps out... Raw carrot and celery with hummus dip in. (as a side note: houmous is how the major supermarkets spell hummus. But I've seen it written as humus or hoummos. Or even hommos, in America. I'm sticking hummus as in Arabic, it its full name is *hummus bi tahini* - chickpeas with tahini.)

On top of this, I'm enjoying more colourful salads, and experimenting with greens and proteins instead of chips and pastry.

I'm also switching some of my drinks. e.g. from red wine to dry rose and from ale to lager... There's not a huge difference here but every little bit helps. See a few examples below.

A bottle of red = 635 calories

A bottle of dry rose = 535 calories

A pint of dark ale = 210 calories

A pint of lager = 149 calories

A gin and tonic 210ml = 170 calories

A gin and slimline tonic 210ml = 115 calories

Here are three of my 'swim recipes'... (enough for two)

An Evening Dip

Something nice and light at night...

Ingredients:

2 x raw salmon fillets, Cajun spice mix, a bag of bean sprouts, a leek quartered in length and then chopped long ways, salt and pepper.

Method:

Heat some olive oil in a non-stick pan.

Add the salmon fillets, skin down.

Add finely chopped leeks.

Cook on a medium to high heat for ten minutes

Sprinkle 2 spoonfuls of Cajun spice over everything. Sear the salmon all over.

Add the bean sprouts and cover the pan for a further 5 minutes.

Season. The salmon should cut like warm butter.

Benefits:

Salmon is packed with vitamin B, great for bursts of energy and heart health.

Bean Sprouts are high in antioxidants which means they can protect you against loads of bugs and even cancer.

Leeks are high in vitamin K – good for strong bones.

Serve this dish up with a smug look on your face and a glass of champagne.

The Butterfly

This, unlike the stroke, is not hard to do…

Ingredients:

2 x 28-day aged fillet steaks (butterflied), 1 x carrot chopped, 1 x parsnip sliced, four mushrooms chopped. Whole black peppercorns (crushed a bit), sea salt, 3 dollops of low-fat crème fraiche and a splash of water.

Method:

Preheat your oven to 180 (fan oven)

Par-boil the veg for ten minutes, then whack it into a frying pan with the olive oil and the mushrooms. Fry up for five minutes.

Put the lot in an oven and keep warm.

Spray the frying pan with more oil. Sear your salt and peppered butterflied steaks, then lower heat slightly and cook each side for…

3 mins: rare

5 mins: medium

10/infinity mins: well done/incinerated

Before taking out of the pan - turn the heat up again and splash in some brandy. Light the fumes and…flambé. Add the crème fresh and stir. Add that splash of water and stir until it turns into a sauce. Remove the steaks. Slice and then add the juice/blood back into the sauce. Boil till creamy.

Benefits:

Low-fat fillet steak is packed full of protein and iron, which prevents anaemia and fatigue.

Parsnips are high in fibre which helps counteract the possible cholesterol downsides of red meat.

Black pepper is a superfood, high in anti-inflammatory, antimicrobial, antioxidant and anti-cholesterol chemicals.

Serve up with the veg, pouring the brandy and peppercorn sauce over the top of the steak.

A Good Ducking

A quacking treat...

Ingredients:

2 x Duck breasts, 3 brockets of broccoli, three splashes of soya, 1 whole red pepper.

Method:

Spray a non-stick frying pan with linseed oil.

Add two duck breasts, skin down. Let them sizzle for 15 minutes.

Then add the three brockets of broccoli (sliced) into the pan.

Followed by one whole sliced red pepper.

Add a few splashes of soya sauce and stir.

Take the duck out and slice. Then put back in the pan and sear.

Add a tiny splash of whisky and light.

Run your singed eyebrows under a tap and arrange the food nicely on a warm plate.

Benefits:

Duck contains Linoleic Acid, which is excellent for repairing and strengthening cells.

Broccoli is rich in vitamin K and calcium. Great for bone strength.

Red peppers are rich in vitamins C and carotenoids, which with help with eye health and fighting off those bugs.

15

Old Bloke looks at the History of Swimming

The history of swimming? I hear you say... Is there such a thing? Scientists don't believe we're natural swimmers and it's possible, at some point, that we were forced into it. Either by the need to gather food from the sea or perhaps to cross some divide on a regular basis.

If we look at our Darwinian ancestors, the great apes, I'm told that they can't actually swim. In fact, zoos have to be careful about putting moats around their enclosures in case they drown. Monkeys, on the other hand, seem to do quite well. The Proboscis Monkey is particularly good in the water, thanks to its partially webbed hands and feet. Different monkey species have been seen swimming underwater to avoid predators, popping up a good sixty feet away.

It's thought that escaping predators may also be a factor in *our* early desire to swim. However, I wonder if there was perhaps a playful element involved. We've all seen pictures of indigenous people in different parts of the world bathing in rivers and children splashing about at play.

Perhaps, over time, kids realised they could float by themselves if they moved their arms and legs in a certain way and then developed a more structured doggy paddle. It may even have given them some esteem in their community and eventually become a 'rite of passage'.

The first recorded swim, so far, dates back 10,000 years. Somewhat ironically, the evidence for this dip in our distant past is to be found in the Sahara. High on the Gilf Kebir Plateau, on the borders of Libya and Egypt, the Hungarian aristocrat and explorer, Almásy László, discovered a Neolithic cave with depictions of people swimming.

The Sahara Dessert during the African Humid Period was considerably wetter and greener than it is today. The cave is featured in the film and book 'The English Patient'.

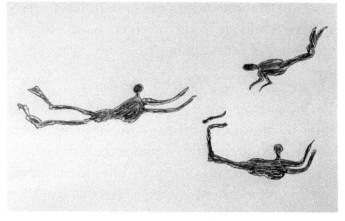

Personally, I'm not sure that the human figures are swimming at all, so let's move on to a more documented age.

The first known swimming pools designed for us to splash about somewhere free of sharks, crocodiles and treacherous currents seem to have been built in what is now modern-day Shri Lanka around the 4th century BC.

However, it was Ancient Rome that gave us a swimming pool that we might recognise today.

They did, however, tend to chuck a few fish in there to spice things up a bit. That is why the Latin word for pool is 'Piscina'. However, it was a chap called Gaius Maecenas of Rome, in the 1st century BC, who built the first heated swimming pool.

The Greeks had them too and both societies made efforts to teach their young boys how to swim. Not very fair on the girls but then no one was back then. In fact, that's still, sadly, a 'work in progress' in some countries.

Fast-forwarding to London 1837 - six heated swimming pools with diving boards were commissioned and more and more people became interested in swimming as a sport.

Pools had also been constructed in America and swimming itself became an official Olympic sport in 1896.

There are now thousands of public swimming pools in the UK and 210,000 private pools. In fact, as the world heats up, it's not only birds and animals that are changing their behaviour, we are too. The number of people building their own pools is on the rise with around 2500 households installing one every year. The U.S. has over 10 million private pools.

Have I thought about building my own pool? Yes, but with quotes well over 50k, I'll leave it until this book makes me *minted*.

Of course, you can 'YouTube it' and build your own pool. This looks to be a more viable option for me, but it's still coming in at 5k or more, so… No. I think I'll stick to my £16 a month at the local authority pool. A bargain if you add it up over the next ten years. And I don't have to clean it or repair it.

I'm writing this book during the Covid pandemic, as pools reopen. So, I decided to look at the degree of 'safety' in an average pool setting.

It's said that Covid is mainly a respiratory infection. That is, it lingers in the air or is passed on by sneezing and coughing into our lungs. So, swallowing someone else's 'gunge' doesn't seem to be an issue. Really? So far, there are no reported cases of pool-driven infection.

After having a chat with a public pool official, it seems that they've almost doubled the chlorine content. A practice that may stay in place for the foreseeable future. They are also trying to upgrade their ventilation systems.

You will also still be required to wear a mask and keep your distance while queuing or walking about in public areas for some time to come…I'm told.

Big Perspex panels separate you from the staff at reception, and most bookings are now online. Many tickets are also collected from a machine rather than a staff member.

User numbers have also been reduced, although you wouldn't know it if you're trying to swim in a straight line.

16

Old Bloke Swims Off into the Sunset...

To sum up, swimming is a wonderful way to exercise. Once you've sussed out the quiet times in your pool, bay or lake, a lot of small strokes just might delay a big one!

It's also a less impactful way to burn calories when you're 'getting on' in years. And, if you're still fit and lucky enough, you might get a chance to pass on your swimming savvy to your grandkids. Or even another old Bloke or old Lass.

I feel much healthier now that I'm swimming regularly. As well as the occasional dip in the sea, I try to do a kilometre in the pool every other day. This, mixed with running between 10k and 20k a week and lots of walking, can't be a bad thing. I'm still reducing my drinking and snacking as best I can. Honest…

I hope you've enjoyed my latest little rant and be sure to put a toe in the water sometime soon. You'll feel so much better for it.

Ciao for now.